This book is dedicated to
family, friends & our teams
who have supported us
on our journey.

Published in the UK by MindBody Publishing

www.MindBodyPublishing.net

ISBN 978-1-8383779-1-5

Design & Illustrations by Âme Connect

ALSO BY THE AUTHORS

Books

Power Up for the Year by Karen Burke

Music

Last Train to Calmsville by Devon Burke
(Magus & Magus)

http://phore.st/52lj8

Products

MindBody Range
Carib Range

http://phore.st/r3Gyf

"It's a new dawn,
it's a new day,
it's a new life for me,
and I'm feeling good."

Nina Simone

CONTENTS

References

Spread the word about the Healing Hug Community

About the Authors

"Breathe. Let go.
And remind yourself
that this very moment is
the only one you know
you have for sure."

Oprah Winfrey

INTRODUCTION

As you enter into this book, take a long calming, soothing breath in…then out, letting it go slowly, allowing you to feel calm, peaceful and to be still in the here and now. Know that there is nothing else for you to do right here, right now this minute…except breathe in a Healing Hug.

Everyone loves a hug! We love giving and receiving hugs and we need hugs especially when we are going through

challenging times. This Healing Hug book gives you tips and techniques on looking after yourself, expressing yourself with the ones you love and also with those in the wider world.

In 2020 when the world was in a different place, we realised how much we missed hugging family & friends and the powerful connection of the human touch. It was especially hard for people who lived alone, the loneliness became palpable.

So, what is a Healing Hug? A Healing Hug can help to give us the strength to carry on. It is the kind of hug shared from one human to another, which fills us up, with feelings of warmth, connectedness, support, encouragement, safety and comfort, the kind we all yearn for.

The Healing Hug is a social interaction which is an exchange between two or more people; the building blocks to society.

A Healing Hug is reassuring and has the ability to convey feelings to someone else. Studies have shown that a hug can help to lower blood pressure[1], slow our heart rate[2] and improve our mood[3]. We tend to relax and drop our shoulders, within a hug with someone close, thus decreasing our heart rate and slowing our breath. It brings a feeling of,

"We're in this moment together"

In this book, we both want to explore and share the different types of Healing Hugs that we have received over the years, especially from our families and friends but also through ourselves; learning to give our own self hug. This is what we call The Healing Hug.

For me, Karen, looking back, I remember Mum's words of comfort she would give

"There, there, don't worry, it will be alright"

whilst patting us on the back and hugging us dearly. On the other hand, Dad would always be the stern voice of reason and wisdom, yet sharing strength, protection and support within his hug.

I believe that I have always given this Healing Hug. It

has sometimes appeared as listening, coaching, teaching, helping people, praying with people or building people's confidence but it has always been there.

For me, Devon, it was developed from within, not knowing my parents until I was 10 years old I had to love me because as a youngster, it felt as if no one else did. Through stillness: being in the here and now, not living in the past or fantasising about the future, is where I understood that I had to love me for whom I was. I had to give myself a great big Healing Hug,

"There, there, it will be alright, it IS alright."

This is now what we do within our centre so that everyone who comes through the door feels the energy of this Healing Hug, from the scents, to the sounds, to the look and feel of the centre.

Whatever your own history with hugs, good, bad or indifferent, you can take baby steps towards discovering how Healing Hugs can benefit you, your family and the world you live in.

"For there is always light if only we're brave enough to see it, if only we're brave enough to be it."

Amanda Gorman

WHAT ARE
HEALING HUGS?

The word hug means to squeeze, to hold someone tight,
to embrace someone in your arms, to express affection, to
bring a rainbow of colours to someone else's life.

A Healing Hug says you are safe. You can breathe now.
I've got you. It is the human touch we need but it is much
more than that. A Healing Hug is to feel our heart beating
in unity with the other person.

*"Hugging has an intimate nature. It brings together touch,
warmth and smell. Each person is different, so a hug
becomes individualised. Sometimes you get their hair in
your face or you feel their earrings or the hint of coolness
from a watch. These are tiny glimpses and fleeting moments
of who they are." Anna*

A Healing Hug is energy from outside of you
complementing the energy from within you, sharing, and
healing each other at the same time. You could wonder
if it has had any impact on the other person but you may
have done more good than you realise, especially if you
did it with good intent.

To do something with intent is to do something with
eager attention; with purpose. It is to use your thoughts to
create an intention to aim for a determined outcome. For
example:

"Here is my love"

"I support you"

"I wish the best for you"

or one of our favourites *"Here is an injection of strength."*

A Healing Hug with intent is therefore even more powerful than a normal hug. Aim for connectedness, love, support, encouragement and warmth. These types of hugs can also help to ground you, to centre you, to fill you up with the strength to keep going.

Then you can pass this on to someone else, to help them take their next step, even when they feel they can't.

Thus a Healing Hug can help to build life-muscles in yourself and others; to strengthen them for the road ahead. To give them a little reprieve from the harsh realities of life before they go back out there.

"You've got this"

Suggestion

To tap into your energy

Rub your hands together fast, and then pull them apart a little. Now bring them in without touching, back and forth and feel that energy between your palms.

Take your palms and rub them over your forehead to the back of your head as you breathe in deeply and breathe out.

This is a good way to ground yourself but also to realise that this energy is always within you to share with others when you give them a Healing Hug.

Food for Thought

Next time you hug, be present, feel the hug, listen to what you are thinking and be present within that thought, that feeling, that moment, that hug.

"I've learned that people will forget what you said, people will forget what you did, but people will never forget how you made them feel."

Maya Angelou

WHY WE NEED HEALING HUGS

Healing Hugs make us feel good!

A Healing Hug can help us to feel safe, to feel supported, to feel accompanied, so we know we are not alone. It can help us to feel like somebody; like we belong. It can also help us to feel rewarded, justified and loved, as well as building trust and confidence in people and within ourselves.

Many people believe that a hug which lasts at least 20 seconds helps to release the bonding hormone oxytocin which can increase happiness and can help to lower blood pressure[1], slow the heart rate[2] and improve our mood[3]. It could also help to heal sickness, dis-ease, anxiety, stress, loneliness and depression.

When we hug and squeeze tight, we apply deep pressure which is detected by sensory receptors in our muscles, joints and skin. This in turn sends a signal of safety to the autonomic nervous system that it is ok to relax, we can drop our shoulders, it is now safe.

Living in such a fast-paced society, with stress on a high, we interact with people around us but sometimes we can forget to connect properly, to stop and look at each other and to share a bit of warmth and kindness.

A Healing Hug can help to bring down our flight or fight response to give our bodies a chance to be still and stillness is the key because it aids healing wherever it is needed, mentally, physically, spiritually or emotionally. The Healing Hug can bring us a further understanding of how to give of ourselves rather than just to give material things. This giving is deeper and lasts longer, plus leaves a legacy of moments shared between you.

Healing Hugs build that connection: that feeling of togetherness, which can help to heal and neutralise differences. Healing Hugs can help to heal rifts between people and stimulate conversations to improve communication, compromise and commitment.

With Healing Hugs we can discover a new way of viewing the world, giving us a better understanding and connection with the people around us, such as our families and our neighbours.

"You give but little when you give of your possessions. It is when you give of yourself that you truly give."

Kahlil Gibran

HOW TO GIVE A HEALING HUG

Hug with your whole heart, freely, hug with good purpose and intent, thus conveying your message to that person loud and clear. Hug without expecting anything in return.

A Healing Hug is more than just a physical connection. It is an agreement made to reach out, to connect, to show and share support. It's a synergy between your physical being and spiritual being, allowing the rhythm of each to create calm, peacefulness and tranquillity in the atmosphere.

"A Healing hug for me elicits a feeling of nostalgia and warmth" Odelia

To hug is like taking a deep breath and then letting go of that breath, ready to allow the mind and body to slow down, to be still. It is to allow the energy to be exchanged, bringing stillness and just Being-ness. There is nothing to do here. There is no judgement in a Healing Hug… just love.

Suggestion

Next time you hug a loved one, stay in that hug for an extra 5-10 seconds. Let them feel that 'I love you' without having to use the words. Your shoulders will drop as you both realise that you are in this hug for the long haul!

HOW TO ASK FOR A HEALING HUG

When you need a Healing Hug, don't be afraid to respectfully ask for one, especially when you are smiling on the outside but weeping and crying on the inside.

Some people tend to give too much all the time and don't know when to look after themselves, especially when they themselves are in need. Others may not know that you need a hug. It may not be a verbal ask but you can position yourself for a hug or indeed give a hug. By giving a hug you also receive a hug.

The worst they can say is no and it may feel awkward having to deal with feelings of rejection but it can inform you of when to ask next time or indeed who to ask in future.

If you cannot find someone to hug, then you can give yourself a Healing Hug. After all, the relationship with yourself is the most important relationship you will ever have in your whole life.

Suggestion

Next time you feel like a Healing Hug ask someone who is physically there or reach out over the telephone so you can connect with someone who can support you.

Food for thought

Do you notice when people are acting out, rather than just asking for a hug? There are times when instead of asking, we engage in attention-seeking behaviour, when all we may need to do is ask, or position ourselves in front of someone to lean in for a hug or just be kind and give what we are looking to receive…a Healing Hug.

"Kindness is a language that the deaf can hear and the blind can see."

Mark Twain

HOW TO RECEIVE A HEALING HUG

By receiving a hug, you also prepare yourself to give a hug.

Always with kindness, graciousness and a high level of acceptance, as it is a gift from that person to you. It can also give something to them as it is an exchange between you.

Accepting a Healing Hug means you accept them, otherwise they may feel that they are not worthy of giving. Maybe it means more to them than to you, so you also give them that gift of receiving their hug.

Suggestion

Receive with open arms.

NB. There is no right or wrong way to give, ask or receive a Healing Hug.

WHO TO GIVE A HEALING HUG TO

Hug your nearest and dearest. Hug your children. Hug your extended family. Hug your neighbours. Hug your community. Hug the world.

It doesn't always have to be about the physical hug. You can give the Healing Hug through words or acts of kindness such as leaving voice messages for someone to tell them you are thinking of them or sending a small meaningful gift.

You can share kind words with strangers, whether in a shop or on a bus, often without being aware of the impact it has. We walk away without knowing how much we may have improved someone else's day.

Suggestion

Next time you are out and about try smiling more and sharing a "hello" with someone to help make their day.

Food for thought

Make a list of all the people you want to give a Healing Hug to.

DIFFERENT TYPES OF HEALING HUGS

"You alone are enough.
You have nothing to
prove to anybody."

Maya Angelou

HUG YOURSELF

You are not alone. You have you.

We all need balance and reassurance and you can give this to yourself through your own Healing Hug.

A Healing Hug is not just a hug it is a pathway to your inner self. It is feeling the power of the energy within. The realisation of how powerful your touch is, your energy is, how powerful you are as a being.

Hugging yourself in stillness can give you the ability to reach into yourself to find solutions, to find peace and healing. Then, having filled up yourself, you will be able to share yourself and your energy with others.

When there is no one to hug, remind yourself that it is okay to hug yourself, heal yourself, to be still and self cradle until you can receive physical hugs from someone else again. Tears may flow and that is okay, allow them to flow, as a way of cleansing and releasing tension, nervous energy, angst and despair.

Even in those times when you are in the midst of a crowd of friends, the centre of attention or where people are relying on you for their feel-good factor, you may give and smile…give and smile, yet feel empty when you go home to your own space alone.

Remind yourself that you can give yourself a Healing Hug. You are not alone. You have you.

Mindful Awareness While You Hug Yourself

So stop for a moment right now. Take a deep breath. Find somewhere comfortable to sit or lie down.

Become aware of yourself and your space by:

1. Noticing and naming what is around you
2. Touching what you are sitting or lying on
3. Listening out for sounds around you
4. Closing your eyes

Find stillness within you, while you physically wrap your own arms around yourself, hug and squeeze tight, allowing the energy of the earth to hold you. Breathe in steadily for six counts and out for six counts.

Breathe in healing, love, strength, thankfulness and breathe out any energy which no longer serves you, such as, feelings of revenge, anger, disappointment, doubt, fears and unforgiveness.

Breathe in positive chi, meaning life force or one energy and feel that warmth, that aura all around your body. Remind yourself of what you have achieved over the years which you may feel is small. However, others may be looking and admiring you from afar. Remind yourself how far you have travelled.

Remember summer days and that life goes in seasons, each bringing its own beauty. Sit within that and cradle yourself until you once again feel whole.

Morning Daily Exercise

When you wake up in the morning, give yourself a hug first by wrapping your arms around yourself. It will be like you are giving yourself your first treat for the day, not waiting for someone else to give that to you.

Then go to the mirror, look at yourself and say,

"I look beautiful, I feel beautiful, the world is beautiful"

"I'm going to have a good day today"

You could also use words such as,

"Hello you"

"Thank you"

"Give me strength"

"I deserve this"

"You got this"

"It's going to be a wonderful day."

It could include your own religious, spiritual or other words that you feel more comfortable with. Whatever words you choose, let them be uplifting and meaningful to you. Be true to you. This can help to ground yourself each morning before you start your day.

Daily Healing Rituals

Find other ways to 'hug' yourself this week, such as:

- **Running a warm bath at home with candles**

- **Putting a warm scarf or cardigan on to feel cosy, enveloped and hugged**

- **Using a drop of bergamot essential oil (or your favourite oil) on your top, scarf or in your bath which can help you to feel calm and peaceful**

- **Stocking up on your favourite hot drink**

- **Visiting physically or virtually a place where you feel at peace**

- **Hugging a cushion or pillow!**

- **Using a weighted blanket for bed to feel snug**

- **Nurturing an indoor plant such as a peace lily (we love these). It is a source of energy, another life which is there, which can give that great release of good hormones when they start to flower. Also, it is a good reminder to nurture yourself.**

"You're braver than you believe, and stronger than you seem, and smarter than you think."

A A Milne

SELF HUG AT WORK & AFTER

"You've got this."

The need for a Healing Hug at work can be high depending on the levels of stress you have to deal with or indeed how you deal with levels of stress.

Some people in challenging roles such as nurses, teachers or the police who may deal with a high number of people on a daily basis, also have to deal with many different energies and auras throughout their day. It is important to cleanse throughout the day, so it is not constantly draining your own levels of energy.

Other work environments and cultures, even if working from home, means you could be dealing with power hungry people, people who have tendencies to bully, or people who, themselves are highly stressed and tend to take it out on you.

It is important to be kind to yourself and detach yourself every so often to give yourself a literal Healing Hug. This is a way of giving yourself, as we like to call it a 'cloak of protection' against stress, ego and demands given or self inflicted on yourself.

Suggestion

Hug yourself for the slow count of 10 and imagine a cloak, cardigan or jumper that you are putting on and it is surrounding you, feeling that warmth, safety and protection. Tell yourself:

"I've got this" or

"They cannot hurt the real me"

"I'm strong"

"I'm smart"

"I'm okay"

"It's okay"

We all know how important it is to take a lunch break away from the desk or your work station and get some fresh air or mindfully sit somewhere else to eat your lunch, staying present in that moment, savouring each morsel of food. That too is a Healing Hug.

Suggestion

Put your right hand on your stomach and your left hand on your chest.

Take a long calming soothing breath in and slowly exhale, allowing your shoulders to drop. Take another long, calming, soothing breath in and hold, allowing your shoulders to drop even more.

Welcome in peace, harmony and kindness.

Allow yourself to stay in that peaceful zone, with that energy surrounding your whole body, to flow within your body and your mind feeling comfortable and at ease with yourself. Sit still being at one with nature and the earth.

This you can do for yourself at any time of the day to help you:

• De-stress

• Think more clearly

• Come up with solutions

• Restore your peace of mind

• Boost your immune system

• Bring confidence

Food For Thought

Did you know that you can use a 'uniform', one kind of clothes to depict work mode, even for those who don't usually wear a uniform, so that when you finish work and get home, you strip off those clothes, have a shower and symbolically wash off the day's stresses and 'work' mentality. Then you can put on your comfy home clothes, which is another way to give yourself a Healing Hug. It can be the signal to move from CEO, carer, manager, nurse to mum, wife, sister, husband or father.

"In family life, love is the oil that eases friction, the cement that binds us closer together, and the music that brings harmony."

Friedrich Nietzsche

YOUR
PARTNER

A Healing Hug can help to increase a sense of harmony, intimacy, love, and togetherness. This Healing Hug is taking the time to be in the moment, experiencing each other's breath; the rise and fall of the chest as you remember 'I'm home'.

"A partner hug can be a lingering hug, in a space where only you can be: feeling safe, comforted and steadied." Suki

A Healing Hug can help to heal each other if you both allow it, as well as feel closer to each other. It can also help to maintain stability within a relationship when you remind each other that you are a team. If you're feeling distant or times have been tough, then make time to have a hug.

It's a *"we're in this together"* kind of Healing Hug.

Suggestion

Next time you hug your partner, hold them close for 10 seconds more than usual to feel the full effects of a Healing Hug.

Another lovely gesture is to hug your partner from behind, for example, when they are doing the dishes! This type of Healing Hug, can demonstrate intimacy and openness.

Food for Thought

As you read through the differing styles of hugs, notice which ones you use as a couple, how many times you hug and where you could bring more hugs into your lives.

YOUR
FAMILY

A Healing Hug can help to reinforce the togetherness within a family unit: to reconnect and confirm that we belong here. A group hug can be wonderful to share and can often end in laughter as we try to figure out where to put our heads!

Hugging family can be like putting on a familiar item of comfortable clothing which we know we can always rely on to be there for us. If feeling low, we can always grab a Healing Hug, which can help to uplift our spirit. Of course, family comes with love but also arguments and disagreements which are normal!

Suggestion

After any disagreements, always end with a hug. It is very hard to stay stubborn and cross with someone for very long, once you've hugged it out. One of you could always shout out "group hug!", which is the signal to all come together and hug it out!

A Healing Hug to a family member can also help to recalibrate the family after a trauma, drama or family issues, as it can enhance and solidify the family spirit. It can recharge and rebalance the tribal energy within the family, the family ethos and can be a reminder of the strength and support held there.

A Healing Hug can help heal old wounds and bridge gaps. Wounds of life can ultimately shape how you give and receive warmth. It is very easy to clam up and protect ourselves when life events happen which can turn us into bitter, cold resentful beings. This in turn can affect how we hug or don't hug our family over the years, which in turn can affect the next generation on how they feel about hugs.

It is up to us to realise that how we deal with events doesn't just affect us but also our families. We can allow instead for gratefulness, acceptance and forgiveness to be allowed to flourish. Of course it can take time as each season brings its own energy, changing throughout our lives and the essence of hugs can change.

Also, it doesn't have to be your blood family it can be whichever family you call your own, where you can pick up more hugs than in your own family. It is a place where you feel a sense of belonging.

It is never too late for us to start hugging, whichever type of hug we embrace.

Hug each other, then hug each other some more.

Suggestion

At the next family gathering, offer a hug to every single person, where appropriate of course. Linger one more second longer than usual and share a kind word, so they don't think you're weird!

Have a family music time and/or dance session, which can help to ease friction and tension in the air. This can increase a sense of closeness, harmony, fun and laughter, which envelopes us all like a big, fat Healing Hug.

"With every word
we utter, with every
action we take,
we know our kids
are watching us.
We as parents
are their most
important
role models."

Michelle Obama

YOUR CHILDREN

A Healing Hug shows safety, calm, peace, tranquillity, trust, safeguarding, protection and harmony. When we teach our children the power of hugs, we can impact them for the rest of their lives as well as the legacy of their children's children. A Healing Hug says,

"I've got your back; no need to worry."

It can also help us as parents to hug our children, especially when we are going through a tough time and feel the need for human touch to bring us back to nurturing times.

"I really love hugging my daughter, how soft her cheek is. I think she smells like she did as a child, which is so reminiscent of her as a baby, which I miss, so love to still get moments." Priya

This Healing Hug lets them know you love them, shares affection and also re-establishes the tribal energy of the family, so they know who and where they belong.

The sharing could be in physical hugs but it could also be in safe family rituals which reminds them *"I'm home".*

Rituals such as the same routine every day or items left in the same place within the house.

It could also be:

- Familiar smells of often cooked foods

- The family games and in-jokes

- The regular places visited

- The regular bedtime routine

- Things you do before you leave the house

However you display it, a Healing Hug, gives familiarity and consistency to a child. It shows them that they are important, that they are an individual. It leaves open a place for them to cry, to recuperate, to allow them to share their feelings. It simply says,

"I'm here."

Suggestion

Share a hug a day with each child in your life. Spend a little longer with them in that moment, giving them your full attention, looking them in their eyes and connecting.

Place your hand on their chest to help bring calm and share things which went well that day. It is a great reminder to stay mindful and grateful.

"You are the bows from which your children as living arrows are sent forth."

Kahlil Gibran

YOUR TEENAGERS

If you've taught them about Healing Hugs, building the routines from when they were younger, they can go off hugs for a while but they will always know where to come 'home'.

Trying to keep giving Healing Hugs throughout teenage years can be like getting on a train without knowing the destination. You never know what mood they are in so you could end up in Edinburgh, Manchester or Liverpool!

"When the world is cruel to them and they need a safe space, the Healing Hug is good for them. Even when they don't know that they need it, you still give them a hug. In the midst of their belligerence, when their face is like stone and their body stiff, it still conveys your presence and love."
Dahlia

This is where faith and trust comes in. To have a strong belief that if we consistently show them love and acceptance, they will feel it, hear it and know it.

To hug as they get older reminds them that we are still there even when we may not like them, their friends, what they are doing or how they are being, in that particular phase of life.

Sometimes, whilst respecting their space, you can give out an invitation to hug to see if they respond. Try not to get disappointed with any rejections but continue to make the effort, offering the hug, so that they know you are always there.

If they are uncomfortable with the full Healing 'bear' Hug, then you can also hug with words or do a hand on heart gesture hug or Wakanda. This is also where a silent hug works very well, sending with intent, thoughts such as,

"I'm still here"

"I love you"

"I'm here when you need."

"Lots of people want to ride with you in the limo, but what you want is someone who will take the bus with you when the limo breaks down."

Oprah Winfrey

YOUR FRIENDS

A Healing Hug with a friend is like an exchange of trust, reinforcing that we are there for them no matter what. It gives and gains trust. It is a reconnection physically and spiritually. Giving a Healing Hug to a friend says…

"I'm here for you, I got your back."

"I am your friend, I support you."

"Take a part of my energy and strength until we meet again."

When you are unsure whether to give a hug but you are feeling kinship, maybe start with an invitation to hug, to see if they are willing first. Then see what kind of hug would be acceptable.

It may change like the changing seasons depending on where they are in that particular moment in life. However a Healing Hug can still do wonders, even when you have no more words or there ARE no words, as your reach out, listen and be there for a friend.

Suggestion

Think about who your true friends are and reach out, rekindle and reconnect.

"The greatness of a community is most accurately measured by the compassionate actions of its members."

Coretta Scott King

YOUR COMMUNITY

The Healing Hug says this is who I am: I come with my arms open and my heart full of compassion. It is an invitation, an open book conveying "I'm not here to hurt you".

It says, "namaste", I bow to you. It acknowledges me, it acknowledges you. We meet on a level playing field. I have nothing to hide. Trust me. We are the same.

Even in big cities we have villages. A village is who you move amongst in your circles. A hug can reinforce and support that village; that community. It can enhance the bonds within your local community. People who were strangers become a member of your village and as energy crosses over they share that same spiritual connection; the village ethos.

This becomes your outside tribe; the people you see regularly who could irritate you as well as uplift you.

These bonds could be experienced at your walking club, school mums café meet up, business support team, your team at the office, your gym club, your neighbours, the shop keeper, the bus driver, your local gift shop or the post person. It can even be experienced amidst nature if we choose to hug a tree.

It is not everyone in our community we can hug or even want to hug. So, a polite hug could be effective, when you're not too sure of a person!

However a simple nod of the head or "hello" can make an invisible person, feel visible.

A Healing Hug is like Reiki (channelling energy through touch or non-touch), passing energy to each other more than just verbal words. Your mood affects someone else's, so intent good thoughts and experiences for people in the community because after all, it is also your community.

Suggestion

Next time you go out into your community:

- **Acknowledge somebody with a wave, a smile or an 'hello'**

- **Stop and talk to somebody**

- **Hug someone who is more familiar to you**

- **Leave a word of kindness**

- **Share a smile**

   These are a lovely way of giving community Healing Hugs.

"What can you do to promote world peace? Go home and love your family."

Mother Teresa

YOUR WORLD

What is your world? Surely it starts with your family, your home, the place you live on this planet.

"I share my love with you. Only the best of what I have, I share with you…to help heal the world, one hug at a time. I give you my best intention." Ekon

Imagine if that was the intention of all of us, every single day, how much love there would be in this world! Sometimes, we may feel that there is no love when bad things happen and the world seems cruel. However, we believe that love and kindness is here in abundance, if we just keep our eyes and hearts open.

The Healing Hug could be a symbol for hope and peace, a sign of welcome, a sign of spiritual agreement, a sign that we are the same and that across the world we all yearn for that same human connection and touch.

The connection we feel then may depend upon our daily attitude towards people other than us, who look different from us, speak a different language, who act different from us. If we stay aware that we are all human beings, capable of communicating with each other, it is amazing how much we could break down barriers. Our own energy is powerful and is able to pick up on someone else's aura even without knowing their language, thus being able to reach out with a kind smile, touch or gesture which in turn can help to encourage togetherness rather than otherness.

We all hold the key. Don't we have a responsibility in however big or small 'our' world is, to approach it with a great big Healing Hug?

Could a simple Healing Hug really help to heal the world? Maybe…we think it can. We think it can be done through one person at a time, in the part of the world that we all live in.

Each one, touch one.

Food for Thought

What if we could help to heal the world, starting with our world…what if we simply started with a smile?

"When you are enthusiastic about what you do, you feel this positive energy. It's very simple."

Paolo Coelho

BEAR HUG
warmth & affection

The bear hug is one of the most popular types of hugs in the world and usually involves the whole body, increasing the positive energy in the atmosphere. It is a big tight, close hug, with arms held wide and around the other person's body, usually held for more than three seconds. You can sink into this type of hug.

This Healing Hug is to give to and receive from someone you love and can ultimately help lift your mood and release pent up feelings and emotions.

"[A bear hug] is like a big tight hug from someone you love; it is the greatest feeling." Funke

"I love a bear hug, when you squeeze tight...very cuddly. It makes me feel loved, warm, emotion and affection. When I feel low it makes me feel better." Maria

"Bear hugs are for family and close friends only." Greg

This is where the Healing Hug really comes into its own with all its benefits.

Science says that a hug which lasts at least 20 seconds helps to release the bonding hormone oxytocin which can increase happiness and can help to lower blood pressure[1]; slow our heart rate[2] and improve our mood[3]. It can also help to heal sickness, dis-ease, anxiety, stress, loneliness and depression. So, why wouldn't we ALL want to hug more!

Next time you are with someone you can give a bear hug to, squeeze them even tighter and hold them for longer. Let them know how good it is for both of you, including your health!

THE ROCKING HUG

food for the soul

This Healing Hug is when the bear hug is not enough and cannot express how much you may have missed this person.

The bear hug is used but along with it comes a gentle rocking motion to convey…

"I haven't seen you for sooooooo long, I've missed you…"

It often comes with a guttural satisfying noise unconsciously released whilst hugging tight like there is no tomorrow "ahhhh…".

We are hugging like there is 'food' in this hug, where you have been hungry for so long…almost licking your lips as you savour the flavour of this type of hug. Like a mother hugging a daughter after a long time, celebrating; sharing congratulations or lovers reuniting.

Suggestion

Listen to your own internal or external noises next time you rock with someone!

"The first gift of
love is to listen."

Paul Tillich

HUGGING WITH WORDS
soothing voice

To listen to the sound of someone's voice alone could be the only Healing Hug we need sometimes, especially on a sad occasion or special day.

Especially if a hug is not physically or practically possible, you can hug them with encouraging words such as:

"You are A-mazing"

"I appreciate you"

"You have my support and love"

"I'm rooting for you"

"I'm here if you need"

"I'm sorry"

"I've got you"

"I Love You"

Whether the words are soothing, lively, funny or just sharing how your day is going, it can help to make someone's day.

Suggestion

**Send someone a word or voice message.
Pick up the phone and speak to someone.
Tell someone how you feel or
what difference they have made in your
life. Tell them today.**

VIRTUAL HUGS
thinking of you

During the 2020 pandemic most of us were forced to stay at home as much as we could, making hugs outside our home almost impossible. Technology was now, not just important for relatives and friends on the other side of the world but for those just a few streets away.

Virtual hugs were given and received through the screens of our TV, phone, PC's and laptops, where the most we could do was pretend to squeeze them virtually & visually with a Healing Hug. We remembered how nice it was to see each other's faces even across a screen rather than just talk over the phone.

You may have sent or delivered small gifts to convey your love, which were received with gratitude when people realised they were in your thoughts.

Others realised that sitting down to take a meaningful phone calls was just as lovely as when the phone used to be connected to the wire in the wall and you HAD to sit in one place!

Lots of us connected by voice notes over messaging apps, again realising how powerful it was to hear a voice during lonely times. Whilst others reached for their emails to connect or even went back to letter writing to add an even more personal touch.

Suggestion

When you think of someone who might need a Healing Hug, send them something such as:

- **A word message or actual voice note**
- **An email from you or forward an email which could help**
- **A written letter and/or card**
- **A small gift**
- **A prayer**
- **A picture, emoji or GIF**
- **Send a funny video to cheer them up**

Food for Thought

We can get even better at giving virtual hugs: sharing the love we feel even when we are tired and busy. Schedule in the love!

SILENT HUG

i see you

When there are no more words, the silent Healing Hug can say things you may not be able to express in words or when words get lost in translation causing confusion and misunderstanding.

It could just be a wink and a smile as a form of connection.

Or it could be any type of hug, be it a bear hug, pat on the back or one arm lean in hug as long as it conveys affection, love and presence.

It can be reassuring and comforting to know that someone is there even if they don't know what to say.

ONE ARM HUG
gentle comfort

This can be a gentle comforting hug where your head leans into the crux of someone's arm for closeness and support when you are comforting a friend. Or between partners, children, grandchildren and teenagers it can be as a means of touch to keep a connection going, to help strengthen the bond.

It is similar to a popular one in Wales called a cwtch (to pronounce it you rhyme it with 'butch'). It means a cuddle or hug but it's a loaded with a comfort type of hug. You wouldn't cwtch just anyone, it's usually reserved for family, or those people who need a bit of TLC. Its second meaning is a cubbyhole, a small space to put things safely - so combine the two and you can see the intention, especially when someone makes a cosy space under their arm for you.

Within an intimate relationship it can develop into a cuddle involving stroking and caressing, leading onto other exciting affectionate bonding activities!

INVITATION TO HUG
establish boundaries

This type of lean forward 'as if you are going to hug' can be used when the other person is an acquaintance or on a date where boundaries have not yet been established.

The invitation to hug is a slight lean forward to hug, to see if they respond or not. If they respond a quick polite 'pat on the back' hug may be okay.

Some people may not be used to touch to show affection and it can be awkward to lean in to hug when they do not respond.

If they do not respond, maybe resort back to a hug with words as in "Stay safe" or "All the best" or use elbows as a means of touch and connection.

PRETEND 'POLITE' HUG

social expression

A polite hug can be the most awkward. It is a half hug, possibly with just one arm, almost meaningless, though could be used by those uncomfortable with a full bear hug or lean in hug.

It could also be without the pat and expressed as an air kiss as you lean in as a way of greeting such as with a colleague or distant relative that you are unfamiliar with.

"Polite hugs are the least favourite of all hugs, Air kisses or quick snatches of a hug where you'd rather really not but you bow to social conventions. Social hugs remind me of awkward silences." Kara

This may not seem like a Healing Hug but due to social interactions can happen a lot more than we expect. It still shows an acknowledgement of the other person as in

"I'm a person too", "I'm in this space with you, see me."

LEAN IN HUG (SHOULDERS)

common ground

This is more of a hug than a polite hug but before a bear hug, where the top part of the body gets close to each other, shoulders touching and could accompany a one pat on the back to show solidarity. Usually more than an acquaintance, it shows familiarity and a common ground.

During 2020, this came into effect, whilst we had our masks on, leaning our heads away, one arm pat on the back as our shoulders bounced. This was awkwardly done around family especially in funerals or at hospitals, where we wanted to show affection but were still unsure of the effects since we had been drilled so much about social distancing.

LEAN BACK HUG
having a laugh

The lean back full body is the lean in with shoulders but instead involves the whole back and possibly bottoms! It can also come with a shimmy up and down if both people are playful and usually ends up in a laugh. This was useful when face to face posed a threat to life, yet we still wanted some touch. It was a way to do a bear hug but back to back.

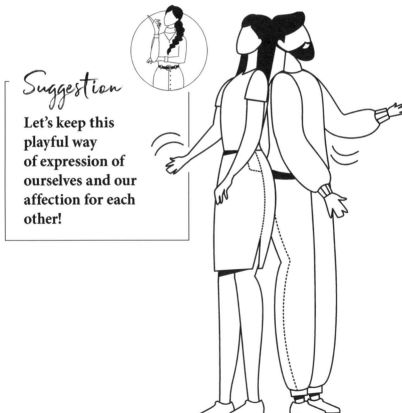

Suggestion

Let's keep this playful way of expression of ourselves and our affection for each other!

HUG WITH ARMS, ELBOWS & FEET

stay connected

Not all done together!

This was another popular greeting instead of a full blown hug, during 2020, when we were told not to hug during the pandemic. We were unsure of the full hug, so reverted to touching with arms or elbows, so that we could still socially distance but enjoy the power of that touch we all so desperately needed. Even the feet came out to play!

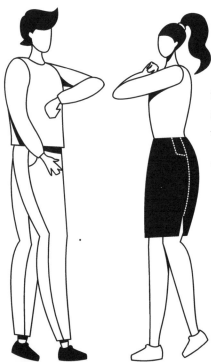

Some touch was better than none,
 for as human beings we
  still need
touch as a greeting,
an acknowledgement, a
way of simply saying.

"Hello, how are you?"

HUG WITH HEADS
deep empathy

This is a gentle touching of the heads as a form of greeting, sometimes with hands on each other's heads or shoulders.

It shows empathy, connection, intimacy, love, respect and admiration. It could also come with deep eye contact. If it feels awkward with your partner, as it is very close, stick with it and see where it takes you.

"Eye contact hug is deep and intimate and not only for partners." Letitia

Suggestion

See how brave you are to do this with eye contact, with a loved one for at least 10 seconds!

BRO HUG
playful behaviour

"...a show of awkward masculine affection." Ekon

If a lean in hug is too much, sometimes even a He-hug will do, which is a very quick bounce of chest and beating of backs. As a male, it says...

"I can hug too. I am physical but I have emotion my brother, however I'm still more powerful than you!"

It is almost a play fight, like rough housing, to engage in rowdy, uproarious playful behaviour, to see who has the strongest grip or pat on the back! This can be a Healing Hug for men in particular, who want to express themselves and show affection.

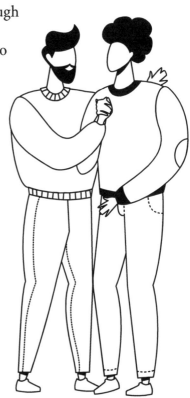

It is still connection and touch in a way that makes them feel safe.

HAND ON HEART GESTURE / WAKANDA

feeling you

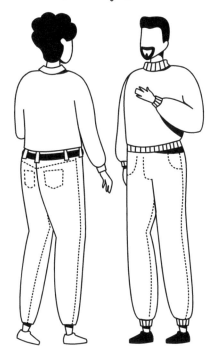

When you want to show affection but don't or can't get close, the gesture of putting the hand on the heart can mean what you want it to mean, from *"I love you with all my heart"* to *"I feel you"* to *"I miss you already"*, especially shown when leaving someone you respect, admire or love.

WAKANDA FOREVER

we are the same

Another sign shown through the popular 2018 Black Panther film, is the Wakanda sign, which took off as a show of solidarity, saying,

"We're in this together, we are the same, I am from your tribe."

A simple nod as you pass one of your tribe on the street can also have the same effect.

FELLOWSHIP HUG
kinship & kindness

Similar to a lean in hug, this one conveys a different message when in the context of a religious setting such as a church, synagogue, spiritual ritual or mosque.

"It is already a community of people with similar beliefs and shows kinship; kindness and of course brings in the human contact." Simeon

It can also be a bear hug to those you love to bits and are familiar with, down to a polite hug or a hand on heart gesture alone, with of course the familiar shaking of hands for those you don't know so well.

Resting in fellowship with each other brings familiarity: the songs, the smells, the worship, feeling safe and held in the arms of something higher than us.

Experiencing the energy of those around us in trance, dance, song or prayer, it raises our vibrations and can send us to higher levels of exhilaration, peace, joy and happiness.

It can take us into a safe space, womb like as we help to heal each other and ourselves. We are saying,

"We're here together, we support you, we are family, we pray with you."

Suggestion

Next time you pass a place of worship and can go in, slip in and sit still for a while, thinking or praying whatever you will and taking in the peace or ecstatic sounds depending on where you are. Note how it makes you feel and ask yourself why.

Rest in that revered state of peace, humility and gratitude as you feel the calming effect of that Healing Hug.

"Every moment is a fresh beginning."

T S Elliot

SAFE HEALING HUG

respectful agreement

A hug should be an agreement between people. It is respectful to gain that permission before we go in for a hug. Thus the varying levels of hugs, which some people may be more comfortable with than others. This also includes knowing when it is appropriate to hug in a work or professional setting or due to safeguarding boundaries e.g. in a school or youth club.

Some people may not have good intentions, so it is important for us to listen to ourselves and follow our instinct that if something doesn't feel right. Stop. Put your arm out as a barrier or step back so that the message is received.

It is a person's right to take a hug or leave it. Rejection can open up other emotions of: not feeling good enough, unloved, unwanted and unsupported. We can then hug ourselves.

So, when a Healing Hug is being offered to you and it feels safe, try to accept it. Even in the middle of an argument, where issues have not been fully resolved, it can bring forth an agreement that "I'm still here for you" or "we are in this together."

Suggested Healing

Choose to forgive yourself and anyone else and change the energy around you and them. Change it by recognising any hurt and pain you may have given or received and getting help if you need to talk it through.

Changing the Energy

The use of essential oils or incense can be a reminder to shift your thoughts from anger to forgiveness if that is what you want to do.

To go in further, the use of a sage smudge stick, where it is lit and the smoke used to cleanse a space, can also help as a symbol of cleansing. Out with the old and in with the new. If you cannot allow smoke in the house you can also use a spray[4] made with intent to spray through the space.

"It isn't where you came from it's where you're going that counts."

Ella Fitzgerald

WHEN HUGS GO WRONG

compassion & respect

A Healing Hug can uncover hidden emotions that you or someone else may have been afraid to look at before, which can aid our growth and healing. It can help us to become aware of ourselves, to become aware of some deep yearning or calling we may have. However, when we attach thoughts, such as, ego, judgement, resentfulness and refusing to forgive into the experience, it changes the energy of the hugs.

Ego

When ego gets in the way, a hug can become constrained and false. It can be full of bad intentions and resolve, to not back down, to not compromise.

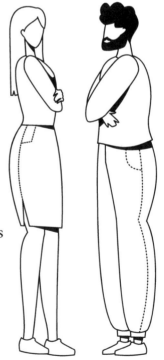

If we can move beyond our ego to recognise and accept the person just as they are, with faults and all, we have a chance to accept ourselves with our own failings. We have a chance to get off our high horse and to hug with forgiveness and a willingness to compromise and accept who we are.

Suggestion

Tell your ego to back down and count to 10, breathing in deeply and out slowly before reacting. Then try hugging the person until both of your shoulders drop and you feel that you can talk freely again with compassion and mutual respect.

Judging someone

Sometimes when we recognise ourselves in others and we do not like what we see, we can act out at the other person. We are then quick to form an opinion about something which may not be so and then refuse to talk about it!

If we can get out of our own heads and stop criticising, we can keep our minds and hearts open to have a conversation before we make assumptions.

Suggestion

Simply listen. Find something nice about the person, yes there must be something! Concentrate on that one thing until you can add another...then another. This helps to ease the negative chatter in our heads.

Resentment

It is so easy to build up an underlying sense of being mistreated or misunderstood by someone, whether it be a partner, colleague, friend, child, parent or manager. Feelings of frustration can build up, some of which may be unfounded until we talk to the person and find common ground again. It can stop us feeling like hugging and send us out of the room rather than into someone's arms.

Suggestion

Have a conversation about it, either in your head to see the full picture or where you could be wrong. Or start a conversation with the person, which could start with something totally different to help ease any tension in the atmosphere first. This is a way to start to move into the Healing Hug.

Forgiveness

It is so hard to stay mad at someone when you are in a long embrace with them, especially your partner. You don't want to back down but one part of you doesn't want to stay mad forever although you may resolve to never do something again within your relationship at that moment! Ego leads to not forgiving the person which can lead to resentment.

Suggestion

Give that person a Healing 'bear hug/cuddle' or 'one arm' Hug for at least one minute so that you both get a chance to calm down. Then… share how you feel or leave it for another day when you are both more susceptible to compromise, love and togetherness.

Funny hugs going wrong

Devon "I remember being young and every time we greeted a certain aunty and uncle; it was always with a French style exchange of kisses. One time, me and my uncle went in to hug and ended up missing the left or right action and nearly kissed each other on the lips! We both saw the funny side of it, never spoke of it but we moved onto shaking hands from then onwards!" Have you ever been in that situation or when heads are banged together because one person came in for a hug too hard?

Suggestion

The Healing Hug is about the intention in those moments. Become aware of what you want your hugs to mean and set your intentions. Whether that be to calm or excite, love, send condolences, congratulations, care or warmth, it is giving the Healing Hug from the heart and ending up in a better place than when you started.

"At the end of the day, we can endure much more than we think we can."

Frida Kahlo

GRIEVING HEALING HUG

lean on me

This Healing Hug could be one of the most powerful touches in someone's life at a time when grief has pierced their heart causing such a tight ball within their chest that they do not know what to do with it or if they will ever heal.

It could be a bear hug with rocking action but here is where your thoughts of intention come into play as if your hug is like a prayer of intent saying...

"I hope you will be alright"

"I wish I could take the pain away"

"I'm so sorry for your loss"

"I'm here for you"

"I feel your pain"

"Lean on me for strength, I wish you all the love and peace in the world"

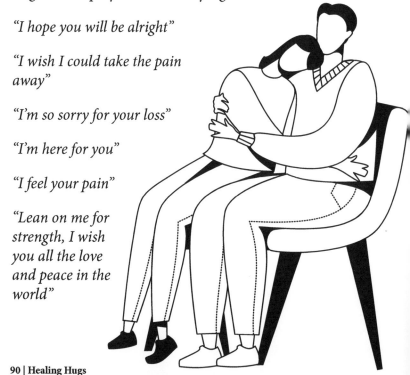

It could lead to a release of emotion from tears to a deep guttural noise of wailing, coming from deep within the person, where from they don't know but you help them to get it out by just holding them tight.

"I've got you"

Some people find it awkward to know what to say during these times but a meaningful Healing Hug can say a thousand words, when your words are choked in your throat and cannot come out. That's okay as it still says,

"I support you"

You may see signs of oversensitivity, absentmindedness, hyperactivity or them becoming a bit more impersonal and stoic. These are coping mechanisms and everyone manages grief in their own way. We cannot hurry the process for them but we can be there giving Healing Hugs.

Suggestion

Give them some comfort by:
- Giving them the Healing Hug
- Baking or cooking something for them
- Helping to clean their place
- Making a nice promise that you can keep
- Sending a word, voice message or picture
- Helping them financially
- Sending a comforting song such as 'How Great thou art' or 'Angels'
- Sharing a collective memory or funny story also helps to relieve pain in that moment
- Booking something in the future, to look forward to
- Making time to listen

"Look deep into nature and then you will understand everything better."

Albert Einstein

HUGGING A TREE

nature's healing

Watching the seasons of nature, can remind us to be patient, that everything happens for a reason, that it all works in synchronicity without us, that nothing stays the same and nothing is wasted.

Through the 2020 pandemic, many of us realised how important nature was to us. We yearned to run or walk outside, to be by running water, to be amidst woodland. In fact, nature came to us in the UK, since it was so eerily quiet during the first lockdown, with nature and animals starting to venture into the streets, wondering if they could claim it back.

Even being close to nature, we are breathing as one. We as humans breathe in oxygen and breathe out carbon dioxide, whereas nature brings in carbon dioxide and breathes out the oxygen we need. We are therefore also receiving a 'breath' hug from a tree. Even when our hands are close to a tree, we can feel the energy if we are still for long enough.

It is okay to hug trees!

Why worry about what anyone else says, as we could be 'off our heads' but we could also be saving our soul by answering its calling to be amongst nature.

Being close to nature is associated with lower levels of

stress, depression, anxiety, high blood pressure, diabetes, asthma, stroke and heart disease.

At the same time, it boosts mood, self-esteem, the working memory and overall feelings of wellbeing. How similar this is to receiving a Healing Hug for 20 seconds or longer!

Our bodies need to go back to nature, to stay close to it, to use any earth we have to grow our own food, to eat off the seasonal land, to eat what the earth gives us, to help save the earth.

Suggestion

Hug more! Go out into nature and experience its natural hug.

Food for Thought

What if we could help to save the planet in our small part of the world, where would we start?

What does a Healing Hug for the planet look like, is it to recycle, re-use, repackage and/or reduce waste?

Being at one with our environment can be like hugging a tree, where we are helping to facilitate the exchange of energy, the synergy between ourselves and the planet and how we exist together. By embracing nature, we embrace ourselves.

"You're off to great places, today is your day. Your mountain is waiting, so get on your way."

Dr Seuss

References

1. Does Hugging Provide Stress - Buffering Social Support? A Study of Susceptibility to Upper Respiratory Infection and Illness - Sheldon Cohen, Denise Janicki-Deverts, Ronald B. Turner, William J. Doyle. First Published December 19, 2014

2. Warm partner contact is related to lower cardiovascular reactivity - Karen M Grewen, Bobbi J Anderson, Susan S Girdler, Kathleen C Light

3. National Library of Medicine - https://nihrecord. nih.gov/sites/recordNIH/files/pdf/2006/NIH-Record-2006-02-24.pdf

4. Safe Healing Hug - See Devon's range of sprays he has created for this purpose, especially his Carib range for sale online http://phore.st/r3Gyf

Spread The Word About The Healing Hug Community

Tap into our websites for upcoming events, workshops and books from Karen and Devon Burke as well as sign-ups for free tools, blogs and downloads.

Buy Karen's Power Up book. http://phore.st/FjupQ

Work with Karen or Devon via 1-2-1 online treatments https://bit.ly/2L3R6mG or via workshops.

Corporate Bookings - MindBody Therapy
https://therapy4life.net

MindBody products are available to shop online such as sprays; smudge sticks, charcoal, resin plus Devon's powerful Carib and Calm range. Look out for Devon's latest #No.1 spray 'Hug in a Bottle'! http://phore.st/r3Gyf

Join in with our monthly One Energy Systems of Healing Reiki sessions where people discuss spirituality, life and also experience group Reiki share.

Events – MindBody Therapy https://therapy4life.net

MindBody Publishing: http://MindBodyPublishing.net sign up for the latest news on books, courses and blogs

MindBody Therapy Business: https://therapy4life.net

Social Enterprise: http://T4H.org.uk

Instagram: MBTherapy

Twitter: @mindbodytalk

Facebook & LinkedIn: MindBodyTherapyCentre

ABOUT THE AUTHORS

Karen Burke, ACMA, MAAT, DipPPC

Karen is passionate about expanding people's self awareness and power, ensuring everyone she works with, has that 'Healing Hug' they need, where she is in their corner, championing them, their career and/or their businesses. She is inspiring, positive, an implementer and loves to multi-task. Her core values are integrity, honesty, loyalty and respect.

She is a business owner, Power Up Coach, Author, Speaker and Accountant, offering Accountancy and Coaching services to individuals and small businesses, looking to start, restart or power up their life and/or business.

Karen F Burke | Twitter | LinkedIn

Devon Burke

Devon believes that we are all spiritual beings on a human journey. His approach is always based in spirituality and that there is only One Energy on earth regardless of what name is attached to it. Above all, it is an individual's intent which shapes and directs their world and outcome. He is a firm believer of Karma that whatever we put out will come back to us in some shape or form, either in this life or another to come.

He has been a qualified Advanced Massage Therapist and Reiki Master for over 25 years. He is a pioneer of the Caribbean Heat Massage©, MindBody Tuning© and the One Energy Systems of Healing©. Devon uses the MindBody Therapy approach. This is a natural approach, which seeks to promote balance and well being to the whole person.

Devon Burke | LinkedIn

"Life is complex within
its simplicity, yet
simple within its
complexity.
B'easy with yourself."

Devon Burke